# OUR NEW BABY

Written and photographed by
JANE HAMILTON-MERRITT

LITTLE SIMON
Published by Simon & Schuster, New York

**Designed by Meri Shardin.**

Manufactured in the United States of America.
LITTLE SIMON and colophon are trademarks of Simon & Schuster..

Library of Congress Cataloging in Publication Data

Hamilton-Merritt, Jane
    Our new baby.

    Summary: Michael adjusts to the birth of a new baby brother and looks forward to being friends with him.
    [1. Babies—Fiction.  2. Brothers and sisters—
Fiction]  I. Title.
PZ7.H182840u        [E]        81-18469        AACR2
ISBN 0-671-44416-6 (LITTLE SIMON)
ISBN 0-671-44885-4 (MCE)

Special thanks

...to all the members of the Michael Woodard and Stewart Snow families who so willingly shared their lives in this book

...to the staff of the Greenwich Hospital Maternity Wing

...to the staff of Sturdevant's Photo, especially Sandy Dimke

...and to Susan, my creative and always reliable assistant

My name is Michael, and I just found out my mom's going to have a baby. I can't wait to tell my best friend.

"Guess what, Benjie? My mom's going to have a baby, just like your mom did."

Mom lets Annie and me feel the baby in her tummy.

Mom says the baby will be very little. She lets us look at our own baby clothes so we can see just how little the baby will be.

"Annie, Mom's going to the hospital soon. Will she be OK?"

"She'll be fine, Michael. Don't worry. Besides, Aunt Evelyn is coming to stay with us and that'll be fun."

When Mom goes to the hospital, Annie and I wave good-bye and go to bed. I am so excited I can't go to sleep, but I finally do, hoping she'll come back soon with our baby.

The next night, Dad lets us pick our favorite story for story-time. Before he tucks us in, he tells us that in one more day we can go to the hospital to see the baby.

VISITING ROOM FOR
BROTHERS AND SISTERS

At the hospital, there is a special room for children to
see their baby brothers and sisters. Annie and I are
afraid to go in. Finally, quietly, we open the door...

...and there is our new baby! He looks all pink and wrinkly and he doesn't have any hair.

A few days later, they bring our baby home. His skin is really soft and doesn't have so many wrinkles now.

After Clarke is home for a few days, Mom says it's OK
for Benjie to come over. "Benjie, this is my brother."

Things are different around here now that Clarke's home. Annie and I have to help Mom.

Dad and I check on baby Clarke when Mom is resting.

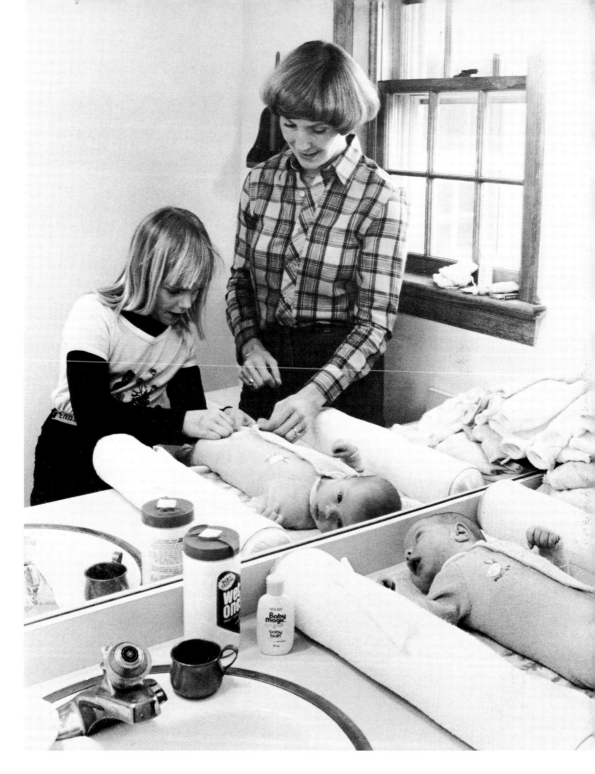

Annie is eight, so she can help change him.

Sometimes, Annie and I fix breakfast and do the dishes for Mom.

Mom says that soon I can feed Clarke. But for now,
I just give him kisses.

One day, I ask my dad if I can take Clarke sleigh-
riding. "Not yet, Michael," he says. "He's too little.
In a few months, he'll be big enough."
It's hard to believe he'll ever be *that* big!

"Benjie, can a baby be your friend?"
"Sure, Michael. I play with my baby brother all
the time."

Zachary, Benjie's baby brother, is older than Clarke, so Benjie can do lots of things with him. Benjie helps his dad give Zachary a bath. Benjie helps his mom feed Zachary. Benjie can even push Zachary in the swing.

When Benjie gets home from school, Zachary's always waiting for him. He's so happy to see Benjie that he squeals and smiles.

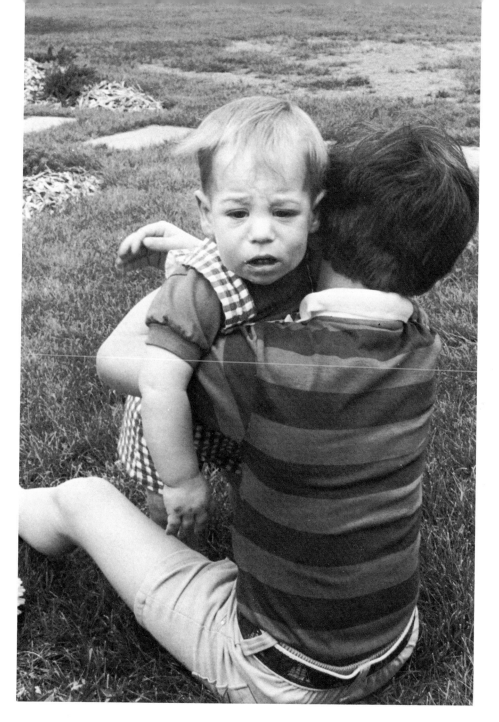

Some days, Benjie says, Zachary doesn't feel like smiling. Benjie says babies have bad days, too, just like we do.

Sometimes, when they play with blocks, Zachary knocks them down. Benjie says it's his job not to get mad.

Zachary even helps Benjie plant his vegetable garden. Benjie says it's fun to do things with Zachary.

Now that Clarke's older, Mom lets Annie and me push
him when we go outside.

Sometimes, Clarke smiles at me and tries to chew on my face. Mom and Dad tell me that even if he's rough with me, I can't be rough with him because Clarke doesn't know any better, and I do.

Annie, Benjie, and I make a cake for Zachary's first birthday party. Zachary doesn't know how to blow out his candles, so we all help him.

Now, Benjie and I both play with our baby brothers.

"You know, Benjie, I'm glad Clarke's my brother.
You were right. Babies can be good friends."